INDELIBLE, MIRACULOUS

Julia Darling

INDELIBLE,
MIRACULOUS

Edited by Bev Robinson
Introduced by Jackie Kay

2015

Published by Arc Publications
Nanholme Mill, Shaw Wood Road
Todmorden OL14 6DA, UK
www.arcpublications.co.uk

Design by Tony Ward
Printed by Lightning Source

978 1910345 30 6 (pbk)
978 1910345 31 3 (hbk)
978 1910345 29 0 (ebk)

ACKNOWLEDGEMENTS
Sudden Collapses in Public Places and *Apology for Absence* were first
published by Arc Publications in 2003 and 2004 respectively.
The early poems first appeared in the following publications:
'Small Beauties' in *Small Beauties* (Newcastle-upon-Tyne
City Libraries, 1988); 'Reminiscence' & 'Gladys' Last Attack'
in *Modern Goddess* (Diamond Twig, 1992); 'Forecasting' &
'Buying Cars' in both *Modern Goddess* and *Sauce* (Bloodaxe
& Diamond Twig, 1994); and 'Men on Trains', 'Good Taste',
'Playing Pool', 'World Cup Summer', 'Be Kind', 'Coming Out 1,
2 & 3', 'Newcastle is Lesbos' & 'Journey with a Golden Lady' in
Sauce.
    The Editor would like to thank Colette Bryce, Linda France
and Ellen Phethean for their invaluable help with putting this
volume together.

Cover photograph: © Sharon Bailey, 2015
Cover design: Tony Ward & Ben Styles

Editor for the UK and Ireland:
John W. Clarke

CONTENTS

FIRST AID KIT FOR THE MIND

APOLOGY FOR ABSENCE

EARLY WORK PUBLISHED 1988–1994

UNCOLLECTED POEMS

Compiling this collection of Julia's poetry has taken me on a journey through our lives, the places we visited, the girls growing up, the years living with cancer and facing death. The poems span from the title poem of Julia's first pamphlet *Small Beauties*, which was published in 1988, to those she wrote in 2005 before she died. Her two books published by Arc, *Apology For Absence* (2004) and *Sudden Collapses in Public Places* (2003) form the backbone of this collection. Prior to these, Julia had published poems in two Poetry Virgins' anthologies, *Modern Goddess* (1992) and *Sauce* (1994). The Poetry Virgins were a performance group that Julia formed with writer Ellen Phethean and actors Charlie Hardwick, Fiona McPherson and Kay Hepplewhite. When I was selecting from these anthologies, I could almost hear the poems being performed and was transported back to rooms full of laughter. Subsequently, some of the poems chosen are those I remember audiences enjoying the most, like 'Buying Bras', 'Newcastle is Lesbos' and 'Forecasting'.

Poems from the *First Aid Kit for the Mind* were originally printed on postcards as part of a collaboration between Julia and artist Emma Holliday. They were included within individual boxes that also contained special and unique objects, like a miniature painting set, worry dolls, and a rubber stamp for your medical notes saying 'I know my body better than you do'. The poems were about living in the 'land of illness' and some had appeared earlier in *Apology for Absence*. This collection has brought together the remaining poems from the postcards and includes 'How to Behave With the Ill' which appeared in the Bloodaxe anthology *The Poetry Cure* that Julia edited with Cynthia Fuller in 2004.

Selecting the unpublished poems was like piecing together a jigsaw puzzle. I read hundreds of poems. Some were early drafts under different titles. A particular line or an image might appear in different poems and I wasn't sure which was the final version. I began to worry whether poems where finished or not, if they were work in progress, and if Julia be would happy about publishing them as they stood. One day I went back to the archive of boxes that contain Julia's work for one last check to see if I had missed any other poetry files. I found a black folder of more poems! Flicking through it, I saw that some were copies of poems already published but at the front of the file it said: 'This file is filled with poems that don't work, or need something! (not all, there are some good ones too)'. There was a list of around 70 poems and in orange ink Julia had marked those that needed work, those she liked, those that had become songs and those that didn't work. This was the guidance I'd been looking for.

Bev Robinson

INTRODUCTION

To say that the poetry of Julia Darling is of great comfort
– to anybody who has ever been ill, or had a loved one
ill, who has had their lives dictated and controlled by a
series of appointments for first one department and then
another; for anyone who has ever had to await the results
of tests, who has had to juggle the paradoxes of complicated symptoms and side effects, who has had their body
altered by operations, their face or hair changed, who is no
longer confident about putting dates in a diary, who cannot now think of a holiday anywhere anymore; for anyone who has had to suffer the length and the length of the
hospital corridor, the patronizing attitude of some doctors
and nurses; who has had to eat and drink things they don't
like and give up practically everything they do; who knows
too well the blood test or the blood transfusion, knows too
well the colour of their own blood; who has had to strike up
a relationship with their illness, personify it, bargain with
it, who has lost days, weeks, years – is an understatement.
Yet what is striking about the poetry of Julia Darling,
collected all together for the first time here, is how, far from
being a bleak and depressing read, these poems charm,
disarm, disrupt, uplift, and surprise the reader.

They are the work of a quirky and original mind, a
charismatic and generous writer and an inquisitive and
enquiring human being who can manage to make the difficult subject of death entertaining and even ordinary. There's
a sharp wit to be found in these poems alongside a tender
wisdom, and there's a mind that is unafraid to take the unexpected turn. These poems invite the reader in; encourage
us to embrace the unexpected, the surprising, the – perhaps
– disappointing. It's as if Julia, in the driver's seat, takes off
at speed, taking the reader on an at times hairy journey full
of hairpin bends and sudden steep hills, laughing, sometimes wildly, then slowing down suddenly to a leisurely

country pace. The reader willingly goes along, because driving with Ms Darling is such fun. That she can move you to tears one minute and the next to laughter is par for the course, and her great strength. You find yourself constantly being caught unawares. You find yourself spotting something you hadn't noticed before.

Then too, there's a great wisdom to be found in the work of Julia Darling. There's common sense advice on how to behave with the very ill, on how to appreciate and live in the moment, in how not to waste time worrying, how to take delight in the simplest of things, how to live your life with as much unexpected elegance as you can muster, how to be defiant and yet glamorous. The poems are jam-packed with a kind of Julia Darling way of seeing the world. They offer up her homegrown philosophy; not only does everything begin with the chopping of an onion, there's no point in worrying about how things are going to end. There is no point in worrying – full stop. 'Beneath your feet the worms aren't worrying.' So these poems, many of them about death, conversely end up turning to life, to life's wonders and conundrums. We end up marvelling at Julia Darling's ability to pull this feat off – to remind the reader how richly rewarding life is, without ever seeming to be judgmental or didactic, to make us want to relish life at the same time as confront the inevitability of death. And life is bustlingly here: cities, civic spaces, lighthouses, families, and holidays. Julia's accurate, beady eye zooms in and picks out details that are fresh, frank and true. The tone of the poems is candid, unfussy, and unpretentious.

Julia Darling had a sunny disposition. I remember hanging out with her on more than one occasion when she was having a blood transfusion. I'd take a picnic – goodies from Fenwicks – we'd play Scrabble, write poems, play Cluedo. Julia noticed what everyone was up to in the ward, and still managed to win everything. I remember thinking I can't think of a single living person that could turn having a blood transfusion into a party. Julia had such a great sense of fun and delight, and this sense of fun is here too and a delight in life's beautiful things, as well as a quiet and barely said regret that she herself will be too early leaving life's great party.

Here are poems that quietly make themselves known, poised, light on their feet, nimble, balancing the surreal with the real; but do not be fooled by their enviable lightness of touch. These are poems that work by stealth, poems that also know how to 'wait beautifully.' They creep up on the reader with their charm, nudge you into thinking – *isn't that it exactly!* They ask brave and deep questions about human beings and how people cope with trauma and stress. But Julia Darling deals as much in death's opposite as she does in questions of health. There are poems that delight in afternoon films, in Sundays, in Newcastle as a city, in macaroons, in frogs, in butterflies, in Englishness, in lesbians, in bra fittings. Self-pity is banished from these poems. There's not one *why me?* Such a stalwart, steadfast lack of self-pity is what makes reading these poems together in this new collection an extraordinary reading experience. The poems take your breath away. They are indelible, miraculous. There's a cumulative experience in the reading of them – even when you were already familiar with many of them. Something about having them all collected into this one volume illuminates the fine and fabulous spirit of Julia, her wonderful decadence, her love of the debonair, her defiance, her willed elegance. Her straightforward no-nonsense approach to everything.

Then too there's the desire to escape; the body is characterised in many ways – memorably as a new extension. The way that realism and surrealism rub up against each other

13

is part of what makes the poems wonderful. At their core, I imagine these poems would have been a comfort to write, but they also let the reader off the hook, 'riding in a chariot made of light… a torch between her teeth.' Darling slices at darkness with her sharp blade. The various descriptions of different people in the book, of her daughters, her partner, her mother, of dentists, doctors, nurses, healers are often psychologically astute and yet sharply observed and original. Who else but Julia would describe someone as 'unemotionally tanned'?

There's a deep and abiding passion here to treat illness differently. Julia was a great champion of how poetry could be used in hospitals, in waiting rooms up and down the country. (She wrote about this in *The Poetry Cure* which she co-edited with Cynthia Fuller.) Julia wanted to use poetry as a medium to help face illness and death and bereavement, to change the way that hospital systems and doctors deal with their patients, to break the mould, to change the vocabulary – not lymphatic, nodal, progressive, metastatic, but lollypop, monkey, lip. You get a great sense here that not only might poetry help heal the reader, but also help heal the writer. The reader gets a sense of the freedom that the poems give Julia from the relentlessness of illness. The writing of the poems for her is a breath of fresh air.

I've spent this past winter walking up and down hospital corridors visiting my parents, who both landed up in Glasgow Royal at the same time. I was reminded constantly of Julia; I even took her advice about walking along the corridors, whilst walking them. My Mum and Dad wrote letters to each other, unable to visit each other, from ward 24 to ward 35. I kept thinking Julia would appreciate that. But my experience this winter also reminded me that, sadly, not enough has changed in the ten years since Julia's death about the way that people are treated in hospitals. And yet the poems were for me again a comfort, reassuringly wise. For every wise word in this book, every moment of truth will often mirror one's own experience too and so the poems become small epiphanies.

Julia and I often went away for a week. We'd hire a house somewhere in the English countryside and read and write. These were such wonderful times; Julia would work away then have a nap, then a boiled egg. And although she was ill much of the time, she never moaned or seemed depressed. She was the very best of company. 'I am not unhappy. I have learnt to drift / and sip. The smallest of things are gifts.' Everything that she learnt from life, from being well and ill, she managed artfully to transform into something useful for other people. There's a sense of the self-unfinished here, of sometimes having to hide behind a mask, of somehow the self still being in the making, needing constructing or reinforcing. 'It's not finished. You can have it when I'm done.' Here's a self that unravels, that does not go to plan. 'Do not plan. Remove all diaries / Be weak. Be languid.' Here's a self that actively encourages people to be whatever they need to be. I imagine these poems being used practically in the way that manuals are used: there's plenty of brilliant instruction in them, to guide us through the dark.

Again and again what you realise is that it is not so much *what* happens in life but *how* you deal with what happens that really matters. 'Sometimes I think there is no such thing as terrible, / only blocked things, lost words, souls that missed the train.'

In the wonderful series *First Aid Kit for the Mind* that came about as a joint art project with Emma Holliday, there's a reiteration of the joy that Julia takes in life, the pleasure in things. I remember these wonderful first aid boxes for the mind arriving finished into Julia's bedroom in her last few days, the late satisfaction she got from the beauty of them, the realisation of an abstract idea into a beautiful thing. I remember hearing Julia read 'How to Behave with the Ill', the nervous laughter of recognition from the audience. Julia, stood, just there, in her long and elegant coat. She had a witty way with the crowd and she put people at ease. No one needed to feel uncomfortable because hers was an honesty that was gentle and delicate as well as bold and brazen. There's a sense in these poems that Julia holds the reader in the same way as she held an audience. The poems are very like Julia. It might seem a funny thing to say but it isn't always the case that poems resemble the poets that write them.

Something mysterious happens in many of these poems. We are often lifted out of the real moment and transported somewhere else. There's an opening of the door of possibilities into a world where people can reinvent themselves, where people are not stuck endlessly waiting. In these poems, Julia takes back the controls, not just over her life, but also over her death. In the last poems included here, the previously unpublished poems, there's a new acceptance of death, and yet even these poems, upsetting as they are to read, are not without hope, without light. There's always somebody shining a torch in the poetry of Julia Darling. And there's always an open window, an open door. And even long after she has gone, she has the last laugh:

Let all my friends say, after I've gone,
'She certainly knew how to die, that one!'

Sadly for us, she did; but her poems know how to live. I hope they have a very long life.

Jackie Kay

SUDDEN COLLAPSES
IN PUBLIC PLACES

HIGH MAINTENANCE

I am walking down a corridor
in the department
for the maintenance
of badly constructed
women.

We have medieval hips
we need scaffolding
we subside.

I have no arches, and my feet
land flat on the wormy floor.
You can hear me coming.
My sockets need rewiring,
there is damp in my wings,
fungi in my joints.

The department is a mess.
There are artificial limbs,
glass eyes, adhesive smiles
piled up. I can spend days
looking for a part.

'It's archaic here',
I say to sweaty
Janet, who searches
in the broom cupboard
for her lost womb.

I bring in flowers,
pot-pourri, room freshener,
presents for the crumpled clerks.
But there is always that smell
of knotted pipes, loose drains,
sickness notes.

I must look hopefully at
the new basin in the Ladies.
And if I sing,
and wear ear plugs,
I never hear the word
demolition.

IMPERSONATION

because I have all day
I take time with
your NINETEEN PAGE FORM
in re-invented handwriting
I write a false name
an invented address
in an avenue
with a view
I find myself sniggering
HA HA this new woman
will unnerve the computer
startle the data base
she will have a doctor
with wings
she will have
no children
no history of diabetes
cancer or mental illness
or a single allergy
no pin number
no postcode
she will have no
category or shoe size
SHE DOESN'T WEAR SHOES
SHE IS A THOUSAND YEARS OLD
her existence will send a thrill
through the corridors
of marketing
like discovering
a Tasmanian tiger
in Northumberland Street
she is as untrodden
as a silky desert
unperturbed as new milk

she was born in a crack
between two millennia
here is my form
I'll tell the receptionist
my smile is a disentangled knot
there goes another one
she'll say, nibbling her nail
they give me the creeps
as if it was that easy
and she'll rip it to confetti
and hand me another

start again properly
Mrs Darling she'll snap
forms aren't funny

A COMFORTING CAR PARK

After the clinic I walk the back way
through the half built wastelands of the hospital
which is riddled with pipes and diggers
and temporary walkways, and rooms ripped
from other rooms, then re-stitched to walls,
ruptured corridors, leading to rubble
and portacabins, crooked signs that point
to ear nose and throat, to amputations
and the Chapel of Rest.

I cut through a car park, into a memory
of outings with my father, to other car parks;
we were going to a tea shop, somewhere
like Petersfield, in the blue Morris Traveller.
He always took us to tea shops, to order cakes.
He didn't make us walk. He hated exercise.
We ate teacakes and jam, got back into the car,
and drove home. Sunned seats warming our legs.

A WAITING ROOM IN AUGUST

We've made an art of it.
Our skin waits like a drum,
hands folded, unopened.
Eyes are low watt light bulbs

in unused rooms.
Our shoulders cook slowly,
in dusky rays of light.
This morning we polished

our shoes, so that they should wait
smartly. Our wigs lie patiently
on our dignified heads.
Our mouths are ironed.

Acute ears listen for
the call of our names
across the room of
green chairs and walls.

Our names, those dear consonants
and syllables, that welcomed us
when we began,
before we learnt to wait.

Call us to the double doors
where the busy nurses go!
Haven't we waited long enough?
Haven't we waited beautifully?

TOO HEAVY

Dear Doctor,
I am writing to complain about these words
you have given me, that I carry in my bag
lymphatic, nodal, progressive, metastatic.

They must be made of lead. I haul them everywhere.
I've cricked my neck, I'm bent
with the weight of them
palliative, metabolic, recurrent.

And when I get them out and put them on the table
they tick like bombs and overpower my own
sweet tasting words
orange, bus, coffee, June.

I've been leaving them
crumpled up in pedal bins
where they fester and complain
diamorphine, biopsy, inflammatory.

And then you say
Where are your words Mrs Patient?
What have you done with your words?

Or worse, you give me that dewy look
Poor Mrs Patient has lost all her words, but shush,
don't upset her. I've got spares in the files.
Thank god for files.

So I was wondering,
Dear Doctor, if I could have
a locker,
my own locker

with a key.
I could collect them
one at a time,
and lay them on a plate
morphine-based, diagnostically,

with a garnish of
lollypop, monkey, lip.

THINGS THAT SHOULD NEVER HAVE HAPPENED

I should never have eaten avocado
or pizza. I should have stayed with pies,

cabbage, neaps. And why did I
travel to Spain and Morocco?

I should have remained on this island
drinking beer, not wine. I should not

have navigated tunnels and crossed bridges.
I was better off in a home made boat

in a small harbour, catching crabs,
boarding insignificant trains, using Tippex.

Carrier bags have not improved my life,
neither has gourmet cat food.

And I could have done without the menopause,
motorway service stations, nylon tights,

long corridors, imitation fires, imported apples.
And the past. I could have done without the past.

SATSUMAS

She is gliding out of Marks and Spencer's
carrying a clematis, a pound of satsumas.
It's just after five. Her legs are heavy.

There is the bus station, green wrought iron,
a woman in blue, selling the *Big Issue,*
a long-coated man with a face like a lion.

She sees the stone angel that flies from a column.
And a child is laughing, a bell is ringing;
the bones of the city breath in a rhythm.

The starlings gather. She peels a satsuma
seeing a bank that was once a tea room,
before that a hairdresser, before that a lane.

She is bulging with maps, with lost streets,
threaded through her like silver. Stone faces
look from the cornices. Perhaps she is turning

into stone? *It's alright,* she says out loud
to the closing shops. *I'm still here. Actually*
dropping her bag of satsumas

watching them fall onto the tarmac, rolling
bright and orange, against the grey.
Living fruit and stone. The kernel of things.

INSOMNIA

Sleep is a friend I have fallen out with,
I wish she would come back to me.

I bring her Valerian, milk and honey
I plead with her, I promise her dreams.

I wander the house listening for her voice
lisping in the cupboards, beyond the walls.

She has sent me here, it's not the same
as the world by day. I have no friends.

I am alone in slumbering rooms
with snoring chairs and bare faced clocks.

I used to love her velvet arms,
her fur kisses, her soundless caves.

If only she would tell me what I've done
and what it is she wants from me.

HEALER

For my healer shall wear pink cardigans,
and she will be called Doris.

And she will live in a bungalow
near New York, which is in Tyne and Wear.

The bungalow shall be placed in the middle
of a windy green field, where cow parsley grows.

And she shall be elderly, and soft,
her wrinkles like mountain streams.

She shall never mention chakras or meridians
and neither will she play whale music.

Rather she will read the Daily Mail
and have poofees and paintings of flowers.

And she will place her eiderdown hands
on my forehead on Wednesday afternoons.

I will close my eyes and hear marching songs
and I shall fear no evil. Even though I walk

through the valley of death.

SQUARE DANCING

I found this square
and in it was my life.
Like a puzzle it divided
different ways,
two triangles or
infinite smaller squares.

There was my corner as a wife,
a deep red square
for all that wine I drank,
rectangular houses, cubes of pain,
squares in which I reared daughters.
That oblong love affair.

In my spare time I cut it out
and stitched it to other squares:
a piece of sky, some matted earth
or thrown-out lives I found in Cancer Care.
If you look, squares are everywhere.
I made a kind of soggy quilt.

I lie beneath it in my room
and spill out beyond
the geometric hem.

WAITING ROOM

I'm waiting for
the drugs to work,
this rain to stop, for results,
the tea to brew,
paint to dry,

for it to harden, to wear off,
my hair to grow, morning,
the weekend, a miracle,
to be put through:

I'm waiting for a ship
to sail up Dean Street.

The right time,
my children to grow up,
for the posse to come over that hill,
I'm waiting for the sequel
and I want to see who wins.

And I'm waiting for
a velvet curtain to rise,
the trumpets, the big drum,
the whole shebang,
a voice from centre stage

calling
over here
this way
it's your turn
now.

DON'T WORRY

about the food you haven't bought,
if your daughter caught that train,
the bill that came, the twinge
in your right leg. Don't fuss.
The washing on the line
will dry again. It's not your fault.
So what if you lied?
Don't be ashamed.

And don't worry that you promised.
It doesn't matter. Let it go.
Just tell her you don't like her if you don't.
You needn't see the doctor with bad breath.
Behave badly. Lie on the floor.
Throw a tantrum if you're bored.
Be late. Be sordid. Eat six pies.
Or trick them by being euphoric.

Above your head a flock of geese
are flying South. Beneath your feet
worms aren't worrying.

LIVING IN THE NEW EXTENSION

First there were plaster bones, pushing through walls
that weren't there before. Sensations like
whirlpools in the lower cellars, a murder of crows

nesting in the parlour. The window frames cracked,
then subsidence; a shifting of deeper foundations
and the drains smelt of another century.

Then, what was once my home was given over
to a team of doctor gardeners, to phantom nurses.
So, I am living in a temporary extension

around the back. It's not what I'm accustomed to,
this quiet, glassy space. A couch. A chair. At night
when they've gone home, with their stethoscopes

and pesticides, I like to wander naked through
the ruined rooms, to smoke, and gaze at all that
space. Recall the wealth I once possessed.

WATER POWER

after visiting Cragside Gardens

I'm harnessing the power of water
like Lord Armstrong who thought,
in a gush of clarity, that water
could make light, and that dim rooms
might be illuminated. So,
I'm imagining light bulbs,
irrigation ditches, and pumps.

I'm opening channels within myself
letting waves swell and break.
It's still primitive. I am conducting
this experiment within a flimsy body.
Conditions are not ideal.
Sometimes all I get is sweat.
But some nights

I'm like Blackpool glowing,
a beacon to myself,
riding in a chariot made of light.
I've got the reins, a torch between my teeth,
slicing at darkness with a blade
riding the current. Some nights I can almost see
beyond, to where the path bends.

VANITY

One day my hairdresser will be an old woman,
her hands leathery from grease, her teeth yellow.

Will I notice as I too shall be old and battered?
Will I still totter to her salon above the travel agents?

Will we strain to see each other in the misted glass?
Shall we still speak hopefully of shape and style?

Or will we be wordless, knowing that the usual
will do? That I'm there to feel the wash

of warm water down my neck, the stroke of fingers,
to be snipped and tidied like a pensioner's garden?

When will it end, this preening and spraying?
This holding the mirror to the back of my head?

DENTAL ATTENTION

In the street of sweets, tangerines and saris,
Mr Mamouji meets my teeth.

He peeks inside as if he's greeting
a room of cautious refugees.

He suggests slow tweaks,
removing ancient mercury,

and talks of roots and my teeth fall
at Mr Mamouji's tactful feet.

They'll be a whitening soon,
a crowning of the feeble ones.

I heard them last night speaking
about him   the relief

of finding a man who understands
their need to speak and to be seen.

WHERE THE LIVING MEET THE DEAD

As it begins to vaguely rain
the narrow lane becomes a track.

I drive on up, until
I reach a man-size hut.

Inside there's a ticket seller
in a blue peaked cap who

sells me an inexpensive ticket
to walk amongst the ruins

where, the guide book says,
the living meet the dead.

I thank him as he lights a cigarette
and watches, unemotionally tanned.

I amble round the overgrown
stones, laced with forget me not and fern

until I find, as I have read,
the door into an underground chamber

where the guide books says
the living meet the dead.

I go inside. There is no light, but then
I see a rustling shape, trembling white:

an American tourist in a mackintosh
sheltering.   Thinking I am come.

THINGS I HAVE LOST

I lost my innocence first,
left it up a tree.
Kept seeing it caught there,
like a balloon,
too high to reach,
too full of air.

Then I lost IT.
IT was the map
you need to get
from room to room.
I lost IT big.

When my education
got mislaid,
I found work
in a laundry
full of white sheets.
I took them home,
played at escape,
death and ghosts.

You can do a lot with sheets.

After that
I searched
and searched
for maturity
which I found
at the bottom
of my mother's
blanket box.

It's tartan.

I put it on my knees.
At night
I watch the news.

By day
I wrap it round my head
and hum,
not harming anyone.

THE BOY'S ROOM

I was tired of my guests
so I wandered upstairs,
found a locked door
at the top of my house
that wasn't there before.

Behind the door there was a room,
rather like a warehouse
full of retro stuff: jukeboxes,
fifties mirrors, cocktail shakers
and lampshades.

The guests followed me,
oohing and aahing,
envying my luck,
touching my things.

Then there was another door
with crooked wooden steps
leading upwards.

I went alone and found
a boy's room, with a boy's
duvet cover and boy's mess
and an untidy wind
blowing through it.

I shouted down at the others
Come and see!
But no one heard
and I felt as if my
head was bursting with ghosts.

I couldn't breathe.

I ran back down.
Come with me to the boy's room,
I implored my guests.
I can't go there alone.

There is no boy's room, they said.
Just this lovely retro furniture.
So desirable. So chic.

MACAROON

I come across rumours about myself
projected onto the walls of the city.
Pale insubstantial ghosts, wordless films,
smelling of damp books, cold as flowers.
I hardly recognise myself. I am bony as a saint,
the colour of tombs. Insubstantial too,
crouching in a bath chair with the nurse who
administers morphine with a delicate spoon.

I must rush to a store to buy lipstick and rouge.
I must never be pale. I smile fiercely. Run.
There are words I must not say: *pain* or *Macmillan*.

But where is the camera? Let me show you
how heartily I can eat this macaroon.

FACIAL

Carol smoothed and rubbed my putty skin
in a narrow room; her hot flannels
circled hollow eyes, she scooped up
sweet, bitter creams. With feather fingers
she massaged my brow, lifted the slack
below my chin. We listened to whales.

When she'd finished she suggested
colour. So I lay there, eyes closed
while she slapped on foundation,
red lips, rouge. And then she left me there,
replenished with a mask of health,
for hours, laid to anxious rest.

AFTERNOON FILMS

Pull me into your bakelite living rooms,
let me smell your leather car seats.

Dress me in a waist, light my cigarette,
curl my hair, paint my mouth, my lashes.

I will wear eau de cologne, have pointy breasts.
Give me a script. Let my eyes shine.

If you pour me a dash, I'll sip and not smudge.
Let me pace your rooms, and never sit down.

Monochrome never bleeds.
My god, I am tired of this sofa.

DOING THE CROSSWORD

A fragment, or a tiny piece of you.
Spectacles slipped down your nose, some tune

whispered from the Philips radio.
Together we gazed at words, brooded

and scribbled in the margins of the news.
The fire fell to ash in the rumpled room.

A flame flared up: a word broke through.
You always got the clues. I'm not sure I do.

THE GROVE

Here is a dusted street in a city,
a fold in the valley, a crease of red brick
threading the bank, a necklace of houses,
strung along by a river, desirable, leafy.

Two girls whisper. Towels flap on lines,
an argument fragments across the vale.
I peer through the glass, down the wild gardens
and dogs look back sadly. Cats stare into ponds.

A child cries and drops a tin bucket.
A man calls his pigeons back to the huts.
Smoke curls from a bonfire, far away there's a siren.
Flowers shudder then close. Someone calls TEA.

When I go, you'll be alone by the window
in this tilting house hanging over the vale,
with the hawthorn, the pond, the rebellious garden,
the light in the evening that fills every room.

OUT OF HERE

I want to build a road
so I'm conversing
with my arteries,
emailing the keepers
of my marshy wastelands.

I want it straight
so I'm dealing with
the mad hill dwellers
who live on the banks
of my lymphatics.

I'm meeting rogue cells
at midnight
in the hot garden
of my heart.

And angel alsatians are
barking at the vandals
who try to
impede construction.

I'm building a road
for a fast car
so I can drive
over that hill
out of here
out of here.

HOSPITAL GEOGRAPHY

In the bowels of this place
a puzzled goddess gazes, frowns
at maps and blueprints of the maze

of geriatrics, noses, ears,
cancers, fractures, X-rays, burns,
brains and hearts, lungs and pipes,

sluices, morgues and casualty,
amputations, things replaced,
and the passages that snake between

the limbs of this enormous thing
that coughs and vomits, bleeds and sleeps
and wails all night for peace.

She sits beneath this rattling mess
and frowns until her temples ache,
pulls out her hair, tries to gauge

probabilities, against the odds
structurally, given every stress
of one harmonious breath.

THE MILL
after staying in A. J. P. Taylor's Mill House, Yarmouth, Isle of Wight

The ferry brings me over the water
opening its iron mouth, letting me
walk back onto the island.

There are stones, then water,
a percussion of ropes and shackles.
Then the Mill, with its long corridors

leading to rooms
I no longer need to visit.
Here the broken bric-a-brac

will never be mended
and armchairs splay out
their horsehair secrets.

Each painting wonders
if it might be valuable
after all this time.

At night Canadian geese
plan their route across oceans
flapping and shrieking.

I sit on the bench,
looking at the simple lines
of the estuary. Children wave

from the silhouettes of boats.
There are footsteps
on the old railway line.

All my history
is simplified to this:
water, stone, flight.

WOODEN SPOON

Here is my grandmother's wooden spoon.
The same spoon that beat its path
through childhood fairy cakes
to a fruity menopause.

Feel its stern handle.
Look into its cracked bowl.
There is power in that worn wood

to make cakes rise, to thicken cream,
to make grown men silent.
This is a working spoon.

Daughter, take this spoon
into your kitchen and stir.

TURKISH BATH

Been squatting in the steam
Been lying on the marble slab
Been hanging out with flesh

Been grunting, been slumping,
Been groaning and farting
Been sweating and lathering

Been grieving and oozing
Been wallowing in the deep tub
Been a jelly, been slack

Been showing my scars
Been with my underbelly
Been right inside my pores

Been scrubbed up, been towelled
Been powder puffed, been oiled
Been got ready, been got ready

VIRGINIA

I've got this friend. She's called Virginia.
I meet her in the seedy parts of rooms.
I disapprove of her; the way she hangs around.
But I can't say no. She needs me. I need her.

I carry her in the pockets of my coat.
I smell of her, of rust and tar and ash.
We're always on the look out for a place
where we can be alone, where we can talk.

I want her like I want to be in love.
There's the rolling, the licking, then the flame,
the thin curl of smoke, the wickedness
reminding me of when our love was hot.

But I deceive myself. She bores me stiff.
Virginia's dreary, sallow and a liar.
Her flaws are many. I can't take her home.
She holds me in her hand and won't let go.

She's a drain. I should give her the push.
My other friends don't understand
why I won't walk away, why I sit
on windy steps when I could be with them.

It's just we go back years. We've had good times.
She's like Judy Garland in the valium days
I can't forget how bright she was and slim.
If I abandon her, where will she go?

I know. She'll vanish in a rattling cough,
leaving nothing but a stub, a nauseous stink,
that some cleaner will briskly wipe away,
and I'll wonder why we carried on this long.

WARD THIRTY-SIX

We are people soaked in onion skins,
arms tied to tubes, in our blue chairs.
The maroon nurse sighs beneath the clock.

The trolley comes, the voice of England
offers Horlicks, sugar, biscuits.
We sip and chew. We place our limbs,

and slump and doze to the beat of drips.
I do the crossword, find new words,
for 'wreckage' and then 'rebirth'.

CHEMOTHERAPY

I did not imagine being bald
at forty four. I didn't have a plan.
Perhaps a scar or two from growing old,
hot flushes. I'd sit fluttering a fan.

But I am bald, and hardly ever walk
by day. I'm the invalid of these rooms,
stirring soups, awake in the half dark,
not answering the phone when it rings.

I never thought that life could get this small,
that I would care so much about a cup,
the taste of tea, the texture of a shawl,
and whether or not I should get up.

I'm not unhappy. I have learnt to drift
and sip. The smallest things are gifts.

SUDDEN COLLAPSES IN PUBLIC PLACES

like buildings, people can disintegrate
collapse in queues, or in a crowded street

causing mayhem, giving kids bad dreams
of awkward corpses, policemen, drops of blood

but I'm stood here, a miracle of bones
architecturally balanced in my boots

I feel each joint, each hinge and spinal link
jolting to the rhythm of my breath

aware of every tremor in my joists,
and yet I'm scared I haven't done enough

to be re-enforced and girded, Christ, I fear
those flowers tied to lamp posts, dread the crash

ANCESTRY

Have you ever seen my extraordinary feet?
They are waders, descended from flippers.
My little toe is related to a prehistoric mollusc.

My legs are Gothic pillars designed in Barnet
by Presbyterians, who sang Jerusalem.
These columns could support cathedrals.

My womb is a wartime nurse,
functional, regular, robust.
A womb that purses its lips.

My belly is the pillow that old ladies die on.
It's Victorian linen, the best in the high street.
It clasps my insides with invisible darns.

My breasts are Scottish, from a line of sepia aunts
who wrapped their bristols tightly in sealy cloths,
with nipples as distant as Iona.

Unfortunately my shoulders are related
to sorry uncles, they hunch and apologise,
sag and wait sadly for sympathetic arms.

But these fine ears are sisters of the sails
that carried cargoes off the flat sea.
They are adventurous and foolhardy.

And this face, that berates me at the hairdresser
and winces in bar mirrors is mine.
I moulded it from ancestral clay.

All mine, with its thumb prints
and crevices. It's not finished.
You can have it when I'm done.

CONVALESCENCE

First you must find a view,
then make a quilt of get well cards
and good wishes. Then unravel yourself,

each knot and tangle, crease and fist.
Undo them. Listen to each limb and crevice,
the voices of your bones,

chart the weather of your body,
the nuances of each breath.
Eat the food of your childhood,

Haliborange and small fingers of bread.
Wear dirty slippers. Forget about words
and pay particular attention to trees.

Be wary of animals and children.
Play Gregorian chants. No mirrors.
Do not wash. Watch insects.

Let things roll under the bed.
Do not plan. Remove all diaries.
Be weak. Be languid.

Flow back into yourself
slowly, tentatively,
when the dust has settled

on the windowsill,
and you have quite forgotten
the colour of work.

END

Eventually, I was placed on a bed like a boat
in an empty room with sky filled windows,
with azure blue pillows, the leopard-like quilt.

It was English tea time, with the kind of light
that electrifies the ordinary. It had just stopped raining.
Beads of water on glass glittered like secrets.

In another room they were baking, mulling wine.
I was warm with cloves, melting butter, demerara,
and wearing your pyjamas. My felt slippers

waited on the floor. Then the door opened
soundlessly, and I climbed out of bed.
It was like slipping onto the back of a horse,

and the room folded in, like a pop up story
then the house, and the Vale. Even the songs
and prayers tidied themselves into grooves

and the impossible hospital lay down its chimneys
its sluices, tired doctors, and waiting room chairs.
And I came here.   It was easy to leave.

FIRST AID KIT FOR
THE MIND

HOW TO BEHAVE WITH THE ILL

Approach us assertively, try not to
cringe or sidle, it makes us fearful.
Rather walk straight up and smile.
Do not touch us unless invited,
particularly don't squeeze upper arms,
or try to hold our hands. Keep your head erect.
Don't bend down, or lower your voice.
Speak evenly. Don't say
'How are you?' in an underlined voice.
Don't say, 'I heard that you were very ill'.
This makes the poorly paranoid.
Be direct, say 'How's your cancer?'
Try not to say how well we look
compared to when we met in Safeways.
Please don't cry, or get emotional,
and say how dreadful it all is.
Also (and this is hard I know)
try not to ignore the ill, or to scurry
past, muttering about a bus, the bank.
Remember that this day might be your last
and that it is a miracle that any of us
stands up, breathes, behaves at all.

HOW TO DEAL WITH TERRIBLE NEWS

Imagine yourself in a space suit, floating through dust,
and that you are the only life on a spinning planet,

because whatever the news, you are still alive
and you can still tell jokes. Tell the doctor a joke.

Or turn back time, and live in a pressure pot of memory.
You can do that. You can ignore calendars and clocks.

Denial is useful. So is a kind of grinning madness.
You are very lucky to live in a warm house, and think

of your vast bath, and the way that you lie in it, gazing
at the clouds shifting, the pigeons flying home. No one

can take that away from you. And your mother.
Not many women have a mother like yours, brave,

original, who tends your universe, and the future.
Sometimes I think there is no such thing as terrible,

only blocked things, lost words, souls that missed the train.

RECIPE FOR A CURATIVE SOUP

All life begins with frying onions,
finely chopped, a few domestic tears,
so start with them.

Then a carrot is a friendly vegetable
easily sliced, bright and optimistic,
colour is the key to everything.

Stir briskly with an opinionated spoon.
Add turmeric, cumin seeds, garlic
and begin to sing

loudly. Sing of pain and new beginnings.
Louder. Pour in the stock from ancient bones,
red lentils, a squeeze of hardened lemon.

Now, drop in a secret. Maybe a word,
a knot of string, a blessing, or a whim.
Stir it in.

Let it simmer like a mountain spring.
Fill the room with soupy love.
Let this be your medicine.

HOW TO NEGOTIATE HOSPITAL CORRIDORS

Don't walk in a straight line, weave your way, grinning
between the abandoned ill, dismayed cleaners, loping porters,
the vats of moving gravy, and the other lost visitors.

Don't glide, or you will feel like a zombie, don't get lost
or you might start weeping, ask every person you meet
if you are heading in the right direction. They will help you.

Stop to look at the art that someone has battled
to hang onto the walls, be an art critic, hum with opinion.
Keep your head up, back straight, collar up.

Halfway down the arterial corridor there's a counter where
a black haired woman sells bacon sandwiches with sauce.
Buy one, and chew it slowly, as you saunter into oncology.

Let crumbs fall lightly onto the polished floor.
They might help you find your way home.

HOW TO FRIGHTEN CANCER

Eat slivers of delicious hams, from delicatessens,
straight from the paper, at bus stops, licking your lips.

Put on extravagant boots with furry trims,
and swishing skirts that flap like owl's wings.

Walk up dangerous paths and gulp down mouthfuls
of galvanising air, raise up your arms and sing,

spread extra jam on everything, arrange red flowers
upon the windowsill. Try not to shrink or moan.

Be big, right up until the end. Don't pull down the blind.
Put on that crazy hat you bought in Spain. And shine.

HOW TO PAINT YOUR SELF-PORTRAIT

Assemble those colours you
once met as a child,
the ochre of a sand pit,
scarlet poppies on her pinny,
grandmother blue, horse
jet, sister yellow.

In the late, sunny afternoon
lay them out in strands,
like wool. Giggle, make
a lovely fussy business of it,
assemble wet brushes, pink paper,
splash water in a glass jar.

Blindfold your old face with bandages
conduct your chicken arm, curse
those rascal cells, uncover
healed scars, hear the orchestra
in the pit, its tubas, it's puffing lips
now your face is a bus route

you can ride your inner self!
Choose carefully where you sit,
count those stops, be
a jigsaw, find out where you fit,
explore the endless range
behind your old snake curtain.

Be surprised by the accuracy of your pain,
thrilled by the face that meets you,
it's so alive, so bright, determined
and now that you've begun
you must start again.
So with a flourish, sign your name.

HOW TO SPEAK TO TIRED PEOPLE WHEN YOU VISIT THEM IN HOSPITAL

Bring unusual gifts, rare ice cream, a dandelion in a vase,
poems, but not the ponderous kind, a box of spice,
things wrapped tightly in tissue and green ribbon.
Talk about the personality of the sky and when there was
another sky like this. Describe horizons, views from trains.
Perhaps the tea trolley comes bumping by, you can
plump the pillows, sort out biscuits, do some
smiling. Once settled with your finger
wrapped around the china handle, you might like
to describe a street before it changed, recall old shops
that sold butter wrapped in tissue, ham sliced off the bone,
loose sweets from jars. This leads quite well to passion
then to love, first kisses, embraces under piers, and lost hearts.
Now you might peel some fruit and eat it slowly.
Allow there to be silence, but keep it fresh.
Now that's enough. Button up your coat, leave like a breath.

APOLOGY FOR ABSENCE

VISUALISATION

You are on a path, leading to the blue wood,
you are floating. Everything you touch shivers
then blossoms. You have perfect knees, glossy hair.
You are sure of your destination (breathe deeply).
You pass a waterfall spilling from a cave
and an elegant fish leaps from the water.
See its rainbow scales. A kingfisher hovers.
Go to the bank, put your hand in the water.
Pure, ice cold water. Wipe it on your lips.
It tastes of honey and elderflower. Drink deeply.
This water will cure you, feel its cool fire
soaking into your bones. You are strong.
Stay there, with the birdsong, don't open your eyes,
for a wrathful cat sits on your chest
and your sheets need washing.
Stay with the path. Keep the nettles trimmed.
Don't think of liver fluke. Try to be American.

WAYS OF DISCUSSING MY BODY

I am a cow, when her calves are taken,
mooing by the gate, with muddy knees.
I'm a woodshed before the explosion,
a swollen kite, pulling at a string.

A giraffe with a narrow and fragile neck,
a still life that's shabbily arranged,
a badly made stool that won't stand up.
I'm that pair of uncomfortable shoes.

I'm a soldier, a veil. I'm a wardrobe.
Do you understand me? I am not what you see.
I am buried at the bottom of a lake.
My parts are many and they don't match.

LIVING IN THE MOMENT

Each moment has edges,
ultimatums, rules.
You can live
in its temporary rooms.

Some moments glitter,
they land in my arms,
red dawns, wild epiphanies.
I have gathered them all,

and stored the best ones
in the safest places
for I may need these moments,
when the present tumbles.

THIS IS A DAY OF SOUP

Luckily, this is a day of soup,
of still surfaces, of back burners,
a day of turning to the small print
and running my finger down a list.
Not a day of suitcases, like yesterday,
of testing handles, the smoothness of wheels,
or a day of corners, steps and slopes.
Last week was all dark tunnels
and lost appointments, fluttering like birds.
Some days are too hot to touch.
I have to wear armour, goggles, gloves.
Tomorrow could be a blind summit.
But today is thick with pearl barley,
lentil and tinned tomato. Today is deliberate,
nutritious. It will take hours,
require a deep bowl, a balanced spoon.

INJECTION

Brown walls. The clip and gleam of hospitals.
Here I am again, having scans, being told
to roll up my sleeve, be still.

And here he is, a freckled man, jabbing at my
hardened arteries, not listening when I say
not that one, that one's dead.

He fails to draw blood, disappears.

In walks a woman with headmistress eyes.
'This one's a squealer', says the nurse,
 so she sighs, rears up with a needle.

I just want to howl for mercy,
to gulp and scream, tell my story,
again and again. Make them sit still, listen.

THE WATER EXTRACTOR

I can't stop thinking about
the water extractor Ann mentioned
as she was going out of the door,
that sucked the moisture out of rooms.

I have tried to imagine
its shape, its vast, thirsty tongue,
the sound of its vibrant recesses,
how it knows not to take everything.

Apparently many machines
are available for hire. Extraordinary.
What other machines are there?
Where is the catalogue?

I would like a spiritual cleanser,
an automatic comforter,
a sushi maker, a cat groomer,
a bath essence maker,

a polisher for my arterial corridors,
a machine for blasting rooms with mirth,
a portable bone strengthener,
and a fear shrinker, one for every room.

GETTING THERE

The yellow number one bus didn't stop
so I crossed the street, boarded a single decker
that lurched out of the ordinary timetable,
faced steep lanes, and terrible bends
that no regular bus could foresee.
I clung to my imagination, my buttons.
My companions had loud conversations
and frail bodies. They hung on, bravely,
as the bus swerved and screamed,
keeled like a boat, shuddered, growled.
We went backwards, we stopped, started.
The bus was filled with leftover people
from other bus routes, other destinations.
We shared toffees. One woman sang.
The journey to the city took so long,
as we made a thousand detours.
I felt that I had seen the universe,
its heights and depressions. I was bruised,
dented with corners, but when I stepped down
the earth beneath my feet felt older, stronger.

EMAIL

How are you? I had a test, but they couldn't find the vein.
How's your pain? Mine's not bad. At night I sweat.
Have you tried those apricot kernels yet?
Mine's round my rib. It hasn't reached the lungs.
Soft is bad. That's what he implied. I'm thinking
if I ignore it, I won't die.

My acupuncturist says I'm doing well.

Afterwards I ate four kiwi, rode my bike.
We always left parties early didn't we? I don't like
hanging round too long. I'm really glad we won't be old
and dribbling in a stair lift, wearing pads.
Have you tried prayer? I never thought I would,
but lately I've forgiven everyone. It's good.

PROBABLY SUNDAY

One daughter is sleeping, her face unbuttoned.
She's dreaming of wardrobes, of sharp gold shoes.

Downstairs her mother writes her will
and studies investments, orders the past.

And the mother's lover is at the computer
shooting dragons and snakes in a watery cave.

Another daughter runs a manicured finger
down a list of queens, memorising their deaths.

The dog barks in the hallway and the cat
examines a spider, then kills it.

We are baking potatoes, it's probably Sunday.
We are an English family in an endless terrace.

SALSA DANCING CLASS. HEATON.

These men that try to dance, whose necks
are wiry red, for whom the steps are
clear as mud. They have a dream

to take off pullovers and swirl, to get
a girl with silver shoes, a jingly belt
which shimmies when she spins. Ah men.

I'm just as bad. I'm stiff meat. But, Mambo beat
I will tame you, flex myself into your Latin
scrum. I've been sofa bound too long,

too fond of being weakly, English pale.
Is it impossible to glow, to wriggle
my backside, click my tongue?

And is it sad, post menopause, to have a whim
to stop doing the aimless Sapphic stomp?
I'll practise, get videos, do anything

to feel a surge, pull out a miracle,
find my Brazil, wake up in Cuba,
plug myself in. Stop counting.

LARGE OLD MEN

The large old men are dancing at a disco
with their wild hands and bowl stomachs.

They stagger amongst the giggly girls
boulders in a river, fallen walls.

They have memories as long as fishing lines
and salt marks on their drooping cheeks.

They are still alive and floating,
bobbing, trying to catch the moths

above their heads. Or waving at the lost
children at the end of the path.

Stamping on the envelopes that came
without warning, those bad letters.

The large old men are dancing at a disco
with their bare faces turned inside out.

PHONE CALL FROM THE HOSPICE

You know when it's Sunday
because the chef isn't here.

Other days are the same,
Pop Idol, magazines.

They fiddle with drugs,
then the visitors come.

Don't worry. I'll get out.
We'll go to Dumfries,

walk down that bright path
to Saint Ninian's Cave,

scratch our names on stones
and place them there.

WHEN I WAS HEALTHY THINGS WERE OFTEN YELLOW

I walked into a town filled with bananas.
The main street was one long banana stall.
It was sweet, rotting, like being
in a milkshake, or being mashed
with a fork, turning brown, ripening.

And I lay on a rug, on pale yellow sand;
dune grass whipped my shins,
the sea was a long devouring wave,
I threw a piece of driftwood shaped
like a sleeping yellow snake.

I was holding a wounded dandelion,
dripping dandelion milk. Its silky head
trembled with a hazy halo of prongs.
It was telling me the time. Buttercups
were knee deep then. Cows were vocal.

I dream of straw, of horse milk,
of the primrose path to the wood,
the vanilla wafer that slipped away.
And fear, a heavy bee against the window,
the tyranny of that ridiculously cheerful sun.

PARENTING

First you were born then
mashed banana turning brown
Barbie's decapitated head
Ken's torso tangled Lego
journeys south a promised sea
adjusting the mirror
share your sweets, sing, sing
wading down copper rivers
wet socks a snow scape out of salt
a door wide open calling down the street
are you coming in, are you, are you?
a gaggle of girls at a bus stop
a bleeding knee wet cotton wool
where's it gone? I want, I want
wrinkled balloons bumping over the grass
at the school fair, primary pastry
clean the paint brushes or they go stiff
a pancake flies into the air
the other mothers in their coats
are you picking up? Or is it me?
sugar oats ribbon rolling eggs
in bed watching Oliver
be quiet go to sleep wake up
a clarinet solo in a school play
that's her, she's mine
crabs in a bucket the boat in the harbour
wiping the kitchen table again and again
fasten your seat belt
passing my credit card across
the supermarket check out
signing my name
is that Ms or Mrs?
many pets all dead
did I tell you I love you?

come back here now!
Then you left.

TURN OFF THE LIGHTS WHEN YOU GO TO BED

I am the woman who wears reading glasses,
listening at the top of the stairs.

I am keeping an eye on your movements,
I know what you eat. I note

the number of hours you sleep, how much
television you watch. I am the night matron

and the day nurse. I hold the keys to your childhood.
I am your worrier. How I worry about your future.

I mould it like clay, but it falls
into pieces in my hands. I tell you be careful,

again and again I say it. Be careful.
Turn off the lights when you go to bed.

Then I monitor your dreams. Madness.
How I wish I would leave you alone.

IMPOSSIBLE

to understand the way a teenager hears questions,
like a whine, disturbing their inner hum.
You have forgotten it, that itching ache.
And the teenager thinks everyone is looking.
It makes them feel as if their limbs are swaddled
and so they hunch their shoulders, lower eyes,
leave the tap running, the top off, slam the door.
They cry, then laugh. They eat without looking
and don't notice the washing in the rain.
You point out that the sink is blocked,
dislike the way they won't keep still.
You want them to be sorry, feel remorse.
But that's impossible, don't you understand?
Because nothing fits, because life is electric,
tomorrow tastes of sherbet, and the night
whirrs round them like a moth, and you
just stand there with your rolled up paper
trying to stop the fluttering, the buzz.

APOLOGY FOR ABSENCE

Look, it's as if my heart is a damp cupboard
filled with old brass that needs polishing.

Or I must cover myself with moss, damp down,
try to establish new growth in the rotting.

Sometimes I am whipped to shreds by the North wind
and must curl up beneath a counterpane.

I need to practise dying, to imagine health,
to eat tinned pears, light unnecessary fires.

And love can be tyrannical, so sweet, yet edgy.
I am overpowered by its fragrant red roses.

Sitting rooms are too vivid. Things get torn.
I have to disappear, to darn each rip.

Forgive me, brave daughters, for the questions
that I have failed to answer. And my love,

please don't say I malingered, don't be
angry later, when you add up the ticks.

AFTER ALL THAT

And then the rooms are empty.
There's a sock on the floor,
a moon-shaped slither of soap,
used cotton wool buds by the bath.

And I have many things to do,
my wiping up, my polishing.
But then, it is also finished
and there is nothing to do.

Why would I want to plant nasturtiums?
For whom am I making a bright garden?
There is nothing I want in the shops.
What is the point of cake?

MY DAUGHTERS READING IN MAY

I love the smell of my daughters reading
as they turn the pages, pushing hair behind ears,
especially in this early summer, with its fat leaves
new and surprised, the trees full of juice
and so many dandelions, so much yellow.
The downy light touches their heads,
their bodies untangle on the long red sofa;
they have forgotten mirrors, clothes, tomorrow.
I could touch their cheeks, as if they were babies,
for they hardly see me as I walk past them.
I can hang in the air, like a comma, breathing,
as their stories unravel, and the afternoon purrs.

SATISFACTORY

The hawthorn outside is shocked with blossom
as we eat a large breakfast. They've got off a ferry,
hair in thin plaits, bent double with rucksacks
as if they still carry the weight of childhood.

Who knows where they've been, with their heavy
tents, and whose mud is crusted on their shoes.
I might pass them in corridors, they wouldn't see me.
They speak a new language of pauses and barks.

I am learning the art of not enquiring,
What is that bruise upon your neck?
Have a tomato. Close the door when you go.
I am off to discover the meaning of ants.

DAYS OF TERRIBLE TIREDNESS

These short days, when I try too hard
to get there, to make myself,

to sit and push, to pull in words
pull up weeds, take vitamin C,

to pedal, to arrive, think it through
to write my lists, tie up ends;

I think sometimes it's finished now,
this endless drive, this pacing on.

I think sometimes I might just sleep
wrapped in fur, close my brown eyes,

be washed away, be satisfied,
with this and what it always was.

SLEEPING IN MARCH

I slept through March; its needling winds
drove me to my bed where I lay with radio plays

and evaporated breath, buttoned in sleep's drowsy coat,
hands clasped on my chest, stone fingers.

I dreamt of missed appointments, failed exams,
while my body folded itself, darned the tears,

sides to middle. Whenever I opened my eyes
the light was fading, only clouds moved.

I felt guilty, as if I was floating out to sea
on a stolen raft, as if my old headmistress

was calling *You lazy girl, you're drifting again,*
you're not even wearing a beret!! I ignored it all.

I slept through March, and rose in April.
My skin had lost its creases. I had new eyes.

SEPTEMBER POEM

On my new bike I will swerve round your corners
dodge your lights, make one way my way.

I'll be a leaf, a glossy conker on a string,
a bright red berry that looks surprised.

Think I'll start a bonfire, smoke all day,
eat blackberry pie, pickle those onions,

hold my trousers up with string, pull
the frayed cuffs of my pullover. Suck wool.

This September joy, an alarming hope,
strong as cider, even though I'm shivering,

smelling the chill, so I keep wheeling
warding it off, whistling, pretending

I have never been cold. Never afraid,
never had to cross the ice.

NIGHT SWEAT

You wake up with your face melting,
an evangelical bird calling you,
the sky dripping with loss.

You claim to be asleep.
Your eyes are closed. Your breath
plods round your chest.

You attempt to plead
with night. You make a promise.
You say that if he lets you go

you'll give him all your furniture,
sew up the arm holes in your clothes,
donate your family to science.

Night covers up your mouth
and nestles in your hair.
He says you have till dawn,

after which he expects results.
The straw must be spun into gold
and you must be able to answer.

MY COMPLICATED DAUGHTER

What can I do for my complicated daughter,
my terror, my dark heart, so lost in this house?
Where can we meet? On the stairs, on the landing?
At night as we dream? In the bold brass of day?
If only I could make her a cagoule of rescue,
heal all her scars, wrap her sore life in silk,
or bury her pain at the end of the garden
with my bare hands. I'd give her a sack full of wishes.
But she will not hear me, and I cannot see her.
We collide in the bathroom, by the terrible mirror,
so apart, so unable to give or receive.

LISTENING TO JACK LISTENING TO MUSIC

After bedtime she closes the door and turns up Joni,
or Kathleen, or Ella. She communes with Nina.

I can hear her chinking, looking into the glass,
searching between notes for a path into night.

She's a party, an orchestra, a clamour and hush,
sweet, jazz thoughts rise and fall. It's their hour,

she's conducting, shushing them, putting them straight.
She won't take them to bed. They might never untangle.

I hear her minors, her majors, her magnificent solos.
Inside the fridge champagne pops by itself.

I am upstairs, dreaming, hearing that magic,
those embers, those divas, singing her home.

NURSES

Slope shouldered, bellies before them,
the nurses are coming, garrulously,
they are bossing me in and out of clothes
into windowless rooms, tucking me in.
Nurses are patting me, frowning,
then they guffaw in another room.
They have flat footed footsteps
and very short memories.

But I am the woman who won't take off her bra,
the one who demands that you look in her eyes.
Miss Shirty, they call me, I know my own veins;
when they come back for me, I'll be gone.

WEIGHT

I am weighed down by carrier bags
of duty, cans of obligation.

A bowl sky sags above my head.
It's like sitting in a tent in the rain.

These blankets are as heavy as cows.
My bones are fossilised trees.

I am clogged up with sympathy,
so that nothing turns or whirrs,

but some things are never onerous
like you in your white ironed shirt

bringing the tea in the morning, quietly
whispering, *sleep, if you want to, sleep.*

TWO LIGHTHOUSES

I would like us to live like two lighthouses
at the mouth of a river, each with her own lamp.

We could see each other across the water,
which would be dangerous, and uncrossable.

I could watch your shape, your warm shadow,
moving in the upper rooms. We would have jokes.

Jokes that were only ours, signs and secrets,
flares on birthdays, a rocket at Christmas.

Clouds would be cities, we would look for omens,
and learn the impossible language of birds.

We would meet, of course, in cinemas, cafes,
but then, we would return to our towers,

knowing the other was the light on the water,
a beam of alignment. It would never be broken.

RENDEZVOUS CAFÉ: WHITLEY BAY

I would like us to meet
where the Horlicks is sweet.

I could tell you my story
with a knickerbocker glory.

Talk of mermaids all day
spooning pear parfait.

Licking ninety-nine cones
we could turn off our phones.

Smile, perhaps disappear,
with a chocolate éclair.

Rendezvous with the sea
and the sugary breeze.

Come eat strawberry flan
while we can, while we can.

OLD JEZZY

I went to old Jesmond Graveyard
to find my plot, to mark a place.
Doug from Bereavement showed me a spot
green and reflective, under a willow.
He apologised for the trimming of weeds,
he liked it messy, overgrown,
but the government had made stipulations
for health and safety, things must be neat,
in case of gravestones squashing children,
so raggy old Jezzy was having a clean up.
But you know, said Doug, death isn't tidy.
It's a plague of knotweed, a bed of nettles,
a path through thistles, that's how it should be.

A SHORT MANIFESTO FOR MY CITY

This city shall treasure its pedestrians
and its small places, its irregular shops.

It shall hang onto its pink lanes, its towers,
Dog Leap stairs and Pudding Chares.

And the city shall never try to be Barcelona,
or dress itself in luxury underwear.

Let it be salty, and rusty with iron,
keep secrets beneath its potent river

And be proud to be radical, afraid
of refurbishment. It doesn't need fireworks,

or Starbucks; for it knows its interior.
Let it always be ready to take off its hat.

My city is hard stone, canny and clever.
Don't give it a mirror. Let it be itself.

MY THUMB IN LEEDS

My thumb is on holiday. It hooks itself
around a key, unlocks a hotel bedroom door.

It lies in green water and softens.
It flicks the remote, orders room service,

says thank you, enjoys being licked.
My thumb puts on its best gloves.

It rides in my pocket. It's pink,
enthusiastic. My thumb takes photographs.

At the art gallery it touches sculptures,
resolves to take up painting, feels my fingers.

Holds a cup of cappuccino, touches clothes
on rails in Harvey Nichols. My thumb sighs.

It carries the cases home, grips on tight.
That's all a thumb can do. Hold on.

MOVING TO THE COUNTRY

We are always looking at for sale signs
down leafy lanes, imagining ourselves
freed from sirens, the clank of the city.
We try to see ourselves in fields
with large deep freezes, happily
wearing floppy hats, with secateurs.
We hope that we would fit in,
with our urban graces, our town shoes,
though the village people scowl
and have thick fingers, hang dead birds
from barbed wire fences.
We would try to trust the animals
who seem so furious and dim.
We would ignore the crows
that arrange themselves like omens.
We always end up driving home, relieved
full of scone, saying we would miss the cinema.

COAT

so I open the door and the air smells
of snails and unwashed flannels and I am
unsure what coat to wear for I might
be too hot in my macintosh or perhaps
rain will slither down my neck in a jacket
so I turn back and go to my wardrobe
and contemplate the rows of coats I keep
huddled there old women waiting for an outing
for I have so many unworn coats

HOLLOW

From the high bed I can see nothing but blossom,
Good Friday light, with a pale egg sky.

It's a simple day, like that flower in a blue vase.
I am a long way from a supermarket car park.

Here in the hollow, with the lull of wood pigeons,
in the open palm of another woman's history.

THE RECOVERY BED

I am lying on a bed in the debatable lands,
considering matters of queenly importance.

The room has two windows, and from each I see
the far far horizon, the reclining hills.

And the bed is decisive, with fine brass bed knobs
and a heavy quilt. It's a bed of grace.

There's no one here. I am able to lie
all day, if necessary, letting my life

fly past like the birds, rise and fall as the clouds;
I am riding a raft that was made by kind women

who have left me here, who gave me a key,
for I was forgetting to look out of the window, but now,

I shall float home, firm as this mattress.
You will find me quite sure, convalesced.

MY OLD FRIEND HOSPITAL

You know the cadence of my footsteps now,
and I am intimate with your sighs,
those humming lifts, your fluttering blinds,
your Fionas, Paulines, Marilyns, Dots,
your *this might hurt, there, all done,*
the swish of your trolleys, your cotton arms,
strolling doctors, the fridge that's full of juice,
the purr of the green curtains pulled
round the bed, the sauntering ward clerks
carrying my thick, buff coloured files,
while my temperature rises and then falls.
Whoever would have thought
I might love a hospital, but I do:
you know me now, and I know you.

IT'S NEARLY TIME

to pull on socks again. A wind
blows exhausted teacloths on the line.
They flap and flap

and all the fields and trees
are wrung out. Their colour has
drained into the earth.

The sky's a sheet in an Oxfam shop
with grim stains shaped
like warring countries.

We must cover up red varnished toes
and hammer down the days
cut things back to stubs,

examine bolts and catches,
stock up on anti-ageing cream,
Solpadine, and learn some jokes.

HEARING THINGS

I heard my insides first, an alarming hum
of swelling pipes, the glug of blood
around my heart, the Gestetner of my brain,
wrench of intestine, whine of bones.

I listened further, to the silence
at the heart of everyone, that wide lake
with guarded fences. I tried to catch
the fishes breathing, bubbles from the deep.

Then, yesterday, in my front room, I heard
the tearing sound of children leaving home.
At the bus stop, there was music in the folds
of a pensioner's skirt, and the high

pitched squeak of longing, a teenager
who held her silent mobile phone
and yearned for it to ring. I wish
that I could hear the future, but I can't.

IT'S NOT OVER

A walk you thought was over
opens into a miraculous valley.
You're in your stride.
You've thrown away
the map and you
could walk forever.

The bush that died
now leaps with blossom,
as if it's dressing for the Oscars.
It isn't cowed by winter, or
newsmen who call through sand
The world is ending!

This is the epic last chapter,
the firework that won't
go out, it just keeps spinning.
After the coffees, they bring out
a chocolate mermaid!
A pyramid of ice!

Glorious undead drunks
still flail and croon
down Northumberland Street.
They dance for England.
Oddly, it's not over yet.
This is the best bit.

INDELIBLE, MIRACULOUS

friend, think of your breath
on a cold pane of glass

you can write your name there
with an outstretched finger

or frosted, untouched grass
in the early morning, a place

where you can dance alone
leave your footprints there

a deep pool of silver water
waits for you to make waves

the beach is clean after the storm
the tide has washed away yesterday

we all matter, we are all
indelible, miraculous, here

**EARLY WORK
PUBLISHED 1988-1994**

SMALL BEAUTIES

Let the milk boil over;
the half-filled tins of baked beans sit on the table,
children scribble on the walls with crayons,
clothes heap in riotous mountains.

I am reading a book.

Let the bells ring, bills lie unopened,
doors slam open then bash shut, letters unwritten,
plants unwatered, bread get hard as a rock.

I am thinking about the moon.

Let the bank get nasty, the grass grow high,
children decorate themselves with lipstick,
build houses within houses in every room,
pee on the floor, pull dolls' heads off.

I am looking for a door.

Oh, come here, you small beauties,
together we shall run across the town moor,
with waving fingers, running for our lives.

You are too small, and too beautiful, to ignore.

FORECASTING

He was a viking in his forties.
Tyne after tyne I said, don't dogger me,
just don't dogger me – but he fishered,
me a single parent with no german bite.

I came to like his humber,
and eventually thames towards him.
Dover and dover
we caught the white of each other's lundy,
throwing all faeroes into the fast net,
deep in our irish sea,
rockallin' and dancin' the malin.
Those were the hebrides years.
Until Cromarty

How I wish Cromarty had not met my viking.

Still only forty, we tyned and doggered,
until my fisher ran out.
And he got his german bite all right,
humbering halfway up the Thames,
waves dover him,
his white in the dark lundy,
faeroes swept from the fast net.

I have drunk the Irish Sea,
hearing him, calling through ships,

Rockall – Malin – CROMARTY!

Thanks Cromarty. I hope you sink,
someday.

REMINISCENCE

on the occasion of my mother visiting Beamish Museum

You were frightened
by the recreated co-operative store
at the living museum

you said
imagine it
the whole of Tesco's recreated
each tin and free offer
the music, the carrier bags
even the shoplifters

and what if they took you
on trips down a lifesize replica
of the M1, in a coach and you too old to stop them
if they took your teapots
and put them in rooms
that smelt of the Thatcher years

poll tax bills lying on the doormat
the door locked twenty times
news of the war on television

those were the days
of the entrepreneur
says the guided talk
marvelling at the antiquity
of your ansafone

far better, you said
to forget…

and shivered

BUYING A BRASSIERE

My mother told me self-esteem
is rooted in a well-built brassiere.
After that a girl should
prioritise her feet.
So I'm standing breast-naked
with Sheila from Lingerie.
She rubs her cool hands
to warm them and wields
a tape measure around my secret skins.
Do you know what I think?
I think in all her smooth experience
she has never seen knockers
as weird as these.
Luminous from darkness,
puckered as jellyfish.
Unrelated spaniels' ears.

She piles up boxes
of hoists and straps
designed by welders
and by lunchtime
we have excavated
a brassiere, which I call
Cleopatra, because it is heroic
with enormous bowls
of fragile lace, and hooks
with black splendid eyes.

Sheila writes the size on tissue paper
for posterity, glad to see
my flat back.

I bool off. Well hung, separated.
And the world is different now.
Even men on building sites
are silenced, in awe
of my magnificent frontage.

BUYING CARS

do not do what I have done
you'll end up lost on the cold M1
or stranded with your big end gone
do not do what I have done

don't trust men with MOTs
who offer Fiestas with guarantees
and never say thank you and never say please
while handing you over the grimy keys

of the shining Fiesta that shudders inside
it's really a Lada with bits on the side
a Frankenstein, with its ends untied
its linings and bearings all tangled and fried

and when you return with a dying car
you'll find that Terry has gone to the bar
and Michael has gone off looking for scrap
and Gary says... they'll phone you back

so zip up your jacket, hold up your chin
and unravel the mysteries of the engine within
study your manual, don't believe him
when he says he's adjusted your steering pin

no, don't believe Terry or Gary or Pete
who hide in the alleys behind every street
join the RAC or use your feet
and buy some spanners... reet!

just don't do what I have done
there's nowhere so lonely as the cold M1
as the hard shoulder with your big end gone
do not do what I have done

GLADYS' LAST ATTACK

Gladys is planning her last attack
she has fought the corners of carpets long enough
tiger memories rustle behind curtains
her haunches spring like oiled caterpillars
she despises the domestic, is mad at this city life
the tin opener, the waiting

her of the wide feet and tangled hair
has forgotten her again
voices speak to Gladys on the ansafone
her fierce head furs up with them
Gladys hurls paper across the room
catching the fluttering wings
with sharp jungle teeth

and at night dances alone on the scratched chairs
quick things dancing on the edges
of her wild green eyes

in this spiderless silence
Gladys plans her last attack
on her, the old lion woman
who limps in, weary of the dangerous world
calling into the cavernous rooms
not knowing that Gladys waits
wild as a stalking leopard
about to stalk up the vertebrae
of her owner's shadow

GOOD TASTE

She wants to wear a torn netting skirt,
a creased and glittering rag
and a plastic flower in her hair.

Just a flower, she cries, *and lipstick
and my angel shoes!*

It's raining, I say, with bad faith.
When you're wet
and your ankles shiver
above insubstantial socks
your flower will droop
and you won't thank me.

But I know
in that other world
there is no cold.
Only the warmth
of other girls' shoes.

All she desires
on a grey January morning
is a bit of glitz,
the stuff that Barbie's made of,
something to flounce.

I catch her tears.
*You are beautiful
without all this paraphernalia.*
But she has slipped off,
stolen lipstick in her pocket,
corned beef legs
against freezing winds,

head aflame with visions of elegance,
dreams of good taste.

PLAYING POOL

We all know
what we're talking about.

The silver is on the table.
The triangle of coloured spheres
will break.

Me or him.
He'll never live it down
if I win.

That's why I'm ambitious and hot
wanting to beat him
black, purple and blue,
playing pool like a boy
with my eyes down
in the low shabby spotlight
of a yellow room.

Me or him.

The male chorus
gurgling on Guinness
hangs from the ceiling.

Balls roll, like the eyes
peering at my arse
as I bend and squint,
arch over backwards
with professional
amateur dramatics.

And pocket mouths
close and twist

as we click on
desperately.

Me or him.

The last ball hangs like smoke,
snookered, caught in its blind trap.

And how they love me when I lose.
They love me when I lose.

WORLD CUP SUMMER

Gawky. Eight. She stares
at a fright of magpie strips
flapping towards her.

Come on LADS!

thunders Coach,
a man whose tea is now baking.
She shrugs, attempting indifference,
lopes to his whistle.

Come ON lads!
Pace. PACE.
Tuck in behind him.
Worry him.

Coach is FIFA, I am Big Jack,
agitated beyond the white line,
longing to run to her
with water.

DON'T JUST STAND THERE, TACKLE!

If football is theatre,
don't let my girl be an understudy.
Coach doesn't hear.
He has made her a sub,
practising skills on the sideline,

and at night she will paste
footballers' shaven faces
into her scrap book,
dreaming of shinpads.

Oh god of football and improbability,
let Ireland win the World Cup.

And let her keep a foothold
on this uneven pitch.

MEN ON TRAINS

The big man who sits opposite
is holding a mobile phone.
He dials a number carefully
and listens to it drone.

Someone answers and he says
Hallo, hallo, it's me.
His voice is oddly dangerous.
I pretend to drink cold tea.

I'm phoning from the hospital
he whines. (We shunt past Leeds.)
*The operation might not work
or perhaps they can cure me.*

Perhaps they can cure me,
he says, nibbling a bit of cheese,
*I just wish you'd phone me up
sometimes. Just once. Please.*

BE KIND

Be kind to white male southern students
who in post–acne anxiousness lumber
down the narrow pedestrian walkway
on their way to slowly open bank accounts.

Be tolerant. Even though they keep
meeting each other, neighing like donkeys,
swinging their half-cut hair and strappy bags
standing in heavy clumps.

Don't think about their parents in Surrey,
or blame them for bending
your windscreen wipers, or roaring rude words
when even the birds sleep.

Or shudder at their purchases in corner shops,
Pot Noodles, Fray Bentos, Vesta and peas.
Or imagine their corner of a communal fridge,
their lonely anglepoises, their non-stick milk pans.

Perhaps they are homesick, worrying about
their parents' divorces, and yesterday's essay.
Or have agonising lovebites on tender shoulders.
Or are wishing they had gone to Exeter or Bath.

So don't attack them on your bicycle,
grazing their shins as you pass,
not saying sorry.

They don't all vote Conservative
and pull their trousers down.

COMING OUT

1

that difficult
morass
the silence
before
saying it

when birds fly
round your heart
and the sound
of kettles boiling
is unnaturally
loud

and you skirt around the kitchen

making odd noises
like words

knowing
that what you want
to say
is both unnecessary
and vital

so that
when you say it
if you say it
you grow wings
and smile
with both the corners
of your mouth

2

after I said it
there was a quietness

a bereavement

a sullen holding back of hands

you said

ah well, shall we go to Bainbridge's then?

I said

perhaps flowers would be in order

but you were dwelling
on difficult aunts
who had the sense
to be spinsters

3

three years on
I still hang on your words

ask me how she is
ask me if we're well

do you know we still
sleep in the same bed?

and what I said in 1991
still holds, was not a phase?

my ex-husband is fine I think
I saw him yesterday

for coffee and yes
we're as friendly as ever

but she is the flame
that won't go out

ask me how she is
ask me if we're well

NEWCASTLE IS LESBOS

Sweating in the Turkish baths
or breast stroking in Elswick pool.
Driving buses, besuited, unrooted,
or regularly walking The Barking Dog.

Browsing in the bookshop.
Camping with Vamps in twilight,
rocking with Doris afterwards.
Teaming into the Tyneside.

Plotting on allotments on Sundays.
Playing footsie in the park,
on television, on telephones.
Flirting in Fenwicks.

Newcastle is Lesbos.
They have infiltrated. Look behind you,
under your desk, in the garden,
in your pink rose bushes.

Sappho, come here on holiday instead.
We are in commune with our own Powerhouse.
Come, give praises to our Northern ladies.

The Heat is On.
There's Spit on our Tongues.
We're best in the West,
Walker or Byker
or cruising the wide waters
of the Tyne.

Remember that nice doctor,
social worker, dentist (dammit)
and the woman who winked at you
by the pyjamas in Marks and Spencer's?

Newcastle is Lesbos.
They seem quite ordinary,
they are quite ordinary.
We are.

JOURNEY WITH A GOLDEN LADY

I want to touch
the golden lady
who has stood too long
alone and cold
above the jewellers

I want to climb with her
up onto the chimneys

in the highest arches
of this bandy city
I will kiss her

like cherubs do

our hearts will hang
like starlings from the ledges

we will step amongst
the chiselled world
of brickies' experiments

stroke the gargoyles
that no one ever sees

climbing the lofty lofts
of an ultimate arch

on our way to heaven
halfway anyway

spiralling
up

UNCOLLECTED POEMS

A HAPPY CHILDHOOD

When I was young I used to open drawers
in College Street; your life was folded there.
I'd reach in with my hungry wanting paws,
take anything I felt inclined to wear.

I knew that yours was mine, and that your things
were free. I could take scarves or foxy stoles,
dress up in pointy shoes, your Sunday Best,
your veils, your musky scents, your silks and voiles.

That's how you always made me feel inside,
as if each drawer in you was open wide.
Even dreams and thoughts were not denied.
I stole those too. You never seemed to mind.

But now I'm old, I know how much it cost.
I'd give it back, but most of it is lost.

BAD PARENT

I have stitched up my mouth
until you do what I say.

You wail my name
and I tell you I am busy.

You want every bit of me
so I give nothing.

You are a sponge
so I am a wall.

SMALL THINGS IN THE CUPBOARDS OF LONG RELATIONSHIPS

The foreign coins we didn't spend,
a once-blown whistle, a fairy light,
a photo fallen from a frame,
(you and I, alarmed, in a gondola).

The things between, the useless scrap
in the cupboards of monogamy;
the dice you rolled, a scrabble Z,
lottery tickets that didn't win.

Immaterial, but gathering weight;
a broken chain, a silver pin,
lidless lipsticks, the Queen of Spades,
bent needles, tiny balls of wool.

Gathering in our itching folds,
dropped like cells, discarded skin;
an argument wrapped in a rubber band,
keys that don't fit any lock.

Where will it go, this anti-matter,
when we are gone, our houses cleared,
these broken pens, clips and screws,
a timetable for the midnight train?

That promise in a golden wrapper,
a baby's shoe, a box of pain?
It will burn down, to sticky resin
be buried in the earth's sore heart,
to weight the world, and keep it steady,
for we held on, and did not part.

RECOVERY

Let me get this off my chest
life's alright with just one breast
as we said one night under a glittering star
a breast in the hand is worth two in a bra.

SUPERMARKET SHOPPING

In the aisles of wishes I am alone with this trolley.
The tannoy plays Satellite of Love, that song,
that I found myself in, in an attic, in a rocket of hope
a sparking circuit, a dangerous thing. And now
I am choosing a washing basket. I am forty-eight.
There's a rip in the pocket of this grey woollen coat.
I am not ashamed of age, or of doing my washing.
I buy unwashed raspberries and unwaxed lemons.
We are all strangers, with deep and frayed pockets.
We still have songs in other universes. Travel plans.

ADVICE FOR MY DAUGHTERS

Don't believe the first things,
don't believe the last things,
believe what you see.

Don't sit too close to drains
or spend too long at a stove.
Always know where the exit is.

Don't store too much.
Know what to give away.
Hold as much as you can carry.

If you have children give them magic,
soft songs, a coin under a pillow,
but don't give them everything.

Sleep in good linen, enjoy the smell of lemon,
breathe deeply, dream deeply,
if you don't know what to do, do something.

Don't diet, or be a martyr.
Life is suffering, but you are lucky
so you might as well be happy.

STORYLINE

Everything goes downhill after the flood.
Our houses tumble down into the vale
and we are forced to move to high rise flats
and to live with the smell of wet wood.

I seem to lose the will to live, how you despair!
The children leave. Their things are drenched.
One joins a silent order, the other turns to travel.
You develop an obsession with solitaire.

Oh dear, not much conflict here. Until
I fall in with a cult I meet at the RVI
and start to believe in sacrifice and hell.
You know there's something wrong,

but the cards won't let you go.
Then in comes a lesbian window cleaner
who sees you there and falls in love.
You are flattered, woken up,

but then you realise that I never sleep,
I smell of sausages and alka seltzer.
You realise I am mad and ill,
and that I've been dancing in the graveyard

several times. For old times sake you
start to pull me in. When I'm at death's door
you realise you love me. A scientist in Texas finds a cure.
We administer it in mid air. The summer dries us out.

The end

SHEEP PRETEND TO BE HAPPY

I had to pack my bones, without them I am an empty
    sack,
but I tried to leave my despair behind, and my stout jaw.

The hotel was made of old armchair and good intentions,
the word quiet mentioned in the brochure, many times.

I hoped for a chic hospital, where sensitivity and calm
were served on toast, where I would come undone.

But it wasn't like that. The place was full of dying cou-
    ples,
and I woke up shouting the word VERDIGRIS,

I found the corridors long, I longed for them to see my
    limp.
I had to lose myself amongst the shabby stories

on the library shelves. I took to ordering through room ser-
    vice,
because the waiters tired me with their winey questions.

If it hadn't been for the orange blossom that lined the
    path
down to the beach, and the dull clank of the doomed
    sheep

on the golden terraces, thinking they were happy,
I might have complained, but instead I learnt a kind of
    patience.

GERANIUMS

Like harsh women
geraniums grow
even if you neglect them

they twist into knots
and drop their thin petals
over my window sill

push out small green leaves
like new children
then ignore them

become all stalk
and not much foliage
their earth cracked

sometimes I pull
out the dead leaves
and encourage them to flower

but they are too dry
for colour, too old
for vanity.

ABOVE ME

A nurses arm.
The arch of the scanner.
A sign that reads
Do not look into the laser,
Radioactive.
The refracted light fitting.
Neon tubes in a sort of case.
The smoke alarm.
The water sprinkler.
Those square ceiling tiles,
with bits notched in, like biscuits.

Air,
my angel relatives

and then heaven.

OPERATING THEATRE

but they are always dying on the stage
having bits sliced off, eyes gouged,

while in hospital they try to keep real death
shushed behind the floral screens

though they tell me in the operating theatre
it's quite beautiful, the way our bodies

open out like flowers, the colours of veins
and intricacies of organs, tissues, bone,

yet the surgeons have no language
for this beauty, no time to write of it

but they would love to take a bow
when the curtains are drawn back.

FESTIVAL MASS

I found myself in a cloud of incense
drowning in a Latin mass, a choir
calling to me, sweet and terrible.

As if someone lifted up a heavy
safety curtain, in a darkened theatre
and released a ball of pink velvet light
that shone all over me.

And on the train home, trees emerged from a dull mist,
like red warriors; cows glowed in the warm sunset fields.
The sea appeared, a red bowl of raspberry juice,
and jet black birds flung themselves into the sky.

But then the curtain dropped
and the sky was flat and dark again

but through the material
it still tried to sing, like an open mouth,
perfectly round and fierce,
but not loud enough
to stop the night.

NIGHT MOMENT

The house breathes. I am sitting in the grey gauze of dawn,
and one bird sings, the cat rears and twists around my feet.

The blue cupboard, the yellow floor, the mosaic wall.
The sweat is drying on my back. I was dreaming of water.

Another night, long and blessed, with always one awakening
as if the house calls me, wants to check I am alive.

A NIGHT OFF

Last night I took an evening off.
I acted light, I stood up straight,
and wore a Barcelona shirt,
smoked in an alley, sipped Highland malt,
reclined in a high backed purple chair,
spooned onion soup. Words fell from my mouth,
like a river, a river of silver salmon,
and the wrinkles fell from my eyes,
and the room loved me, the walls embraced me,
the ceiling tinkled its glass chandeliers.
I forgot my swollen heel, my numb jaw.
I pretended I was in Ireland again.
Still, I left early, slithered out into night,
afraid of the clock, the splintering spell.

DARK AND LIGHT

Dark Tuesday's here. I've fallen through, come loose in bed.
My face aching, ice and nails, my bones are laced with dread.

The radio hums and coos, the Archers argue, I try sending
    texts
to friends beyond this raft, like flares. *When will I see you next?*

But I drift out too far, pulled by the tide, around the headland
    to the bay
in bedclothes wet with sea and sand, fishing for my lost day.

I'm beyond the forecast, and I'm not sure what I'll become.
I have no torch, but I hang on, hoping for an arm of sun.

VANITIES

My body visits me
skin, rumpled, bruised, limp
a pot belly, scarred chest
swollen eyes, an absent bottom
such bony legs, such sore fingers.

Go home.
Send me that bouncing girl
with her lardy breasts
and overgrown valleys.
I want her back.
I love her now.

Can't you see it's snowing
in icy fists. I can't go out.
The girl is lost
I'm trapped inside this
crooked shape. In tight rooms.

Is this it?
A life of looking down
the long garden
at the covered vale
anaesthetised by white
bandaged light.

IT MIGHT WORK

Like my old PE teacher with a cane,
pain comes looking for me, to give me a smack.

Opening doors, whispering my name.
Pain calls me to her grey office.

But pain can't quite nail me down,
I am pleasant but elusive.

And I am elated at the stylish way
I escape the hard stick of pain.

It's hysterical, like being the last girl
in the wardrobe in a game of sardines.

How close she comes to me, with hard
steps and long grumbling breaths. But

there are more tricks in my bag,
like not believing in her, or jumping out

and staring right into her heart until
she turns pale, and breaks. It might work.

TRAVELLERS

Later the ceiling of Paris airport collapsed on passengers
    in transit
but that day you and I were quite safe, bright for the journey.
I think it was spring. We were flying to Rio. We spoke softly,
    in woven sentences.
At home there are many photographs of us, arm in arm,
    suitably dressed
all over the world; on a gondola, a beach in Greece, on safari,
    a bus in Barcelona.
We enjoy phrase books, tickets, hotel lobbies. We delight in
    complimentary soaps.
That's why it's so hard to think of travelling alone, without you.
So unfair, when we could have laughed together at foreign
    angels, glided
open-mouthed along that shining pathway. Crossed the Styx
    hand in hand.
I suppose we might still be squashed by an enormous brick,
    but for now
I am lying in the Marie Curie hospice, and things don't look
    so good.

THE RADIO IN THE MORNING

Melvyn Bragg seems to know everything.
I lie under my red quilt and eat bananas.
I line up my pills. I examine the sky.
He is always digging up facts with his radio voice.
My bones feel ancient, quite prehistoric.
Will they be agreeable today? And will it rain?
Tell me that, Melvyn Bragg. Tell me something
of relevance to this shrunken life.

I DON'T WANT ANYTHING

Shopping has become a vague art, impulsive, rather like
    picking flowers
whilst lost in a wood; velvet coats, egg timers, nail varnish,
    I haunt
the malls and carpets of department stores, I buy a pie
    and eat it
in the street. I don't really want anything. I want a box of
    optimism.
I like to feel the breath of other customers as they pass,
    and to smile
at make up girls behind the counters of Clarins and
    Clinique.
At home my room is full of stuff. It fades so quickly,
    everything.
Some afternoons all I really want is a blue sky filled with
    birds,
or to know that there are still enough frogs in the world.

THINGS I HAVE USED UP

I have personally erased forests with my lust for paper
and I've sapped lakes, used up all the moistness in the leaves
on my thirsty skin. I'm so sorry about the children who must have
sewn my underwear. I wish I could think of something useful
that I've done. I wish I had made the atmosphere
a better place for butterflies. My life has been one long honeyed
slice, and here I am, licking my lips, with nothing to give back
apart from the eucalyptus trees I have planted in the garden.

ENTREATY

Don't let me die in a hospital bed,
where death will be deathly, where death will be dead.
Place me on white cushions, with well-placed lights,
and let death descend in the day, not at night.

Let death be elegant, let death be sweet
let death wear a ball gown, and have silver feet.
Let it be oiled, not squeaking or raw.
Don't let death be a hole, rather a door;

a door with a sign, let me know where I'm going.
Let death be lucid, and let it be flowing.
Let death be a courtier and I'll be a queen,
graciously waving at the place I have been.

Let death be a comrade, let death be a laugh,
let death be like sinking into the bath.
Let all my friends say, after I've gone,
'She certainly knew how to die, that one!'

JULIA DARLING was a poet, novelist and playwright. Born in Winchester in 1956, she moved to Newcastle in 1980. Her first full-length poetry collection, *Sudden Collapses in Public Places* (Arc, 2003), was awarded a Poetry Book Society Recommendation; her second collection, *Apology for Absence* (Arc), appeared in 2004.

Crocodile Soup (Anchor Books, 1998), her first novel, was long-listed for the Orange Prize and was also published in Canada, Australia, Europe and the United States. *The Taxi Drivers Daughter* (2003), published by Penguin, was long-listed for the Man Booker Prize and short-listed for the Encore Award.

She wrote many plays for stage and radio, including *Manifesto for the New City* for Northern Stage, and *Appointments* and *Personal Belongings* for Live Theatre. An anthology of her plays, *Eating the Elephant and other Plays*, was published by New Writing North in 2005; the title play was about breast cancer which Julia was diagnosed with in 1994. An adaptation by Jackie Kay of Julia's on-line weblog *The Waiting Room* was dramatised on Radio 4 in 2007.

Julia was Fellow in Literature and Health at Newcastle University and edited *The Poetry Cure* (2004) with Cynthia Fuller which was published by Bloodaxe Books. She believed that poetry should be part or every modern hospital and 'that poetry can help make you better'. In 2014 Julia was honoured by the Newcastle Gateshead Initiative with a Local Heroes bronze plaque in the city. She had made Newcastle her home since 1980 until she died in 2005. To find out more about her work, or read her we-blog, go to

Julia Darling

www.juliadarling.co.uk

JACKIE KAY, the Scottish poet and novelist, studied English at the Stirling University. Her first book of poetry, *The Adoption Papers* was published in 1991 and won the Saltire Society Scottish First Book Award. Other awards include the 1994 Somerset Maugham Award for *Other Lovers*, and the *Guardian* First Book Award Fiction Prize for *Trumpet*, based on the life of American jazz musician Billy Tipton. In 2010 she published *Red Dust Road*, an account of her search for her natural parents.

Jackie Kay is currently Professor of Creative Writing at Newcastle University and Cultural Fellow at Glasgow Caledonian University. She was made an MBE in 2006 and in 2014 was nominated Chancellor of the University of Salford.

Selected titles in Arc Publications'
POETRY FROM THE UK / IRELAND include:

LIZ ALMOND
The Shut Drawer
Yelp!

D. M. BLACK
Claiming Kindred

JAMES BYRNE
Blood / Sugar
White Coins

JONATHAN ASSER
Outside The All Stars

DONALD ATKINSON
In Waterlight:
Poems New, Selected & Revised

ELIZABETH BARRETT
A Dart of Green & Blue

JOANNA BOULTER
Twenty Four Preludes & Fugues on
Dmitri Shostakovich

THOMAS A CLARK
The Path to the Sea

TONY CURTIS
What Darkness Covers
The Well in the Rain
folk

JULIA DARLING
Sudden Collapses in Public Places
Apology for Absence

LINDA FRANCE
You are Her

KATHERINE GALLAGHER
Circus-Apprentice
Carnival Edge

CHRISSIE GITTINS
Armature

RICHARD GWYN
Sad Giraffe Café

GLYN HUGHES
A Year in the Bull-Box

MICHAEL HASLAM
The Music Laid Her Songs in Language
A Sinner Saved by Grace
A Cure for Woodness

MICHAEL HULSE
The Secret History
Half-Life

CHRISTOPHER JAMES
Farewell to the Earth

BRIAN JOHNSTONE
The Book of Belongings
Dry Stone Work

JOEL LANE
Trouble in the Heartland
The Autumn Myth

HERBERT LOMAS
The Vale of Todmorden
A Casual Knack of Living
COLLECTED POEMS

PETE MORGAN
August Light

MICHAEL O'NEILL
Wheel
Gangs of Shadow

MARY O'DONNELL
The Ark Builders
Those Aprl Fevers

IAN POPLE
An Occasional Lean-to
Saving Spaces

PAUL STUBBS
The Icon Maker
The End of the Trial of Man

LORNA THORPE
A Ghost in My House
Sweet Torture of Breathing

ROISIN TIERNEY
The Spanish-Italian Border

MICHELENE WANDOR
Musica Transalpina
Music of the Prophets
Natural Chemistry

JACKIE WILLS
Fever Tree
Commandments
Woman's Head as Jug

Lightning Source UK Ltd.
Milton Keynes UK
UKOW04f0031220515

252094UK00002B/30/P